MW01103779

The Garden of Your Heart

Cultivating a Relationship with God

Jennifer Garces

Jennifer Garces

All scripture verses are taken from the

New King James Version of the Holy Bible

DEDICATION

Because you loved me long before I could ever love myself, this book is dedicated to the King of Kings, and the Lord of Lords, my Heavenly Father, Jesus.

Thank you for keeping your promise and making all things possible because I believed.

I love you.

Jennifer Garces

CONTENT

Jennifer Garces

MEET THE AUTHOR @

www.GardenofYourHeart.com

Jennifer Garces

GENESIS

Hebrews 1:10 And You, Lord, in the beginning laid the foundation of the earth, and the heavens are the work of Your hands.

Sometimes we need to go back to the beginning. Are you willing?

We read that God created a garden in the beginning. A beautiful and lovely place filled with overflowing abundance; an orchard of seed-bearing plants and every variety of fruit-bearing tree. God looked upon his creation and knew it was good. There he placed Adam and Eve to steward the Garden of Eden.

When I go back to MY beginning, dear reader, there was also a garden. It wasn't the Garden of Eden, but to me, it was mesmerizing and enchanting, an abundant place filled with life and wonder. My garden encompassed a small plot directly across from my little house on Newey Lane. A simple chain link fence was the only barrier containing the tangle of tomato vines and assorted rainbow rows of vegetables and fragrant herbs. When the gate was opened and I was permitted access into my primeval forest, something magical happened. That garden became my personal Garden of Eden.

The man who lovingly tended and nurtured this garden was, surprisingly, not God. (Though in my young mind, only a great creator could build such an astounding agricultural achievement!) His name was simply: Mr. Frank. He had a polish accent and was ancient and knowledgeable. His rough, dry farmer's hands held secrets that were only revealed through his workmanship in the garden soil. Mr. Frank would smile as he placed small, ruby red cherry tomatoes into my palms, and watch my face light up as those sweet little treasures overflowed in my tiny hands. Those jewels were the most delectable things on earth.

Almost half a century later, those unforgettable encounters spark a memory in my soul that I long to return to. The simplicity and beauty of those moments saturate my memories with joyful and endearing thoughts that I long to revisit. I remember my Garden of Eden, dear reader; my Genesis place. It didn't encompass the breadth and width and variety that the original Garden of Eden possessed, but it was captivating and somehow, I KNEW God was there. None of that wonder could have been created without his hand or artistry. That was the sparkle that I felt, that I breath as I ponder and write about those appointments. My first encounters with his Holy Spirit.

Sometimes you must return to the beginning in order to reach your future.

Jennifer Garces

SOIL in the garden

Matthew 13:1-9 [1] On the same day Jesus went out of the house and sat by the sea. [2] And great multitudes were gathered together to Him, so that He got into a boat and sat; and the whole multitude stood on the shore. [3] Then He spoke many things to them in parables, saying: "Behold, a sower went out to sow. [4] And as he sowed, some seed fell by the wayside; and the birds came and devoured them. [5] Some fell on stony places, where they did not have much earth; and they immediately sprang up because they had no depth of earth. [6] But when the sun was up they were scorched, and because they had no root they withered away. [7] And some fell among thorns, and the thorns sprang up and choked them. ⁸ But others fell on good ground and yielded a crop: some a hundredfold, some sixty, some thirty. ⁹ He who has ears to hear, let him hear!"

What type of soil does your heart contain?

The soil of our heart will determine the development, and manifest the fruit, of God's planted seed. **The condition of our heart foretells the abundance of our future harvest.**

God's holy word talks about four different types of soil in the garden, or conditions of the heart.

The Lord said, as the farmer sowed, some seed fell on the wayside and the birds snatched it up.

Webster's Dictionary refers to a wayside as the edge or border of a path or road. In the Greek language, a wayside is defined as a literal way, road, or even belief system. Clearly, the soil on the wayside is well travelled, compacted and perhaps even paved. The heart of the wayside is hard, dry, and impenetrable. Seed cannot be received by the hardened crust of the wayside. It lays exposed and uncovered on the surface of the soil and is readily devoured, trampled, or washed away.

*The Lord said to Thomas, his disciple, in John 14:6, "I am the **way**, the truth, and the life. No one comes to the Father except through Me."*

The heart of God is fertile and rich. As we connect with our father in the garden, the soil of our own hearts becomes workable and enriched. As he tills our hardened hearts and makes them pliant with his grace and everlasting love, the Lord prepares a place for his glorious seed to grow and flourish.

Until the soil of our hearts is prepared and ready to receive the message of life, the seed will fall on the wayside. Hearing the message without sowing it is opportunity missed.

Working the soil of our hearts, dear reader, is a personalized process since we all possess unique types of soil. In the garden, it may take several seasons to build a sustaining and viable soil. This holds true for the soil of our hearts. Have patience, dear reader, with the process, and trust in the master gardener.

The Lord said, as the farmer sowed, some seed fell on stony places, where it did not have much soil, but it immediately sprang up. Unfortunately, when the sun rose, it scorched the seedlings because they had no root, and they withered away and died.

Initially, the rocky soil receives the word of God with excitement, and it germinates. As the setting is momentarily just right, the seed begins to grow. Joy and enthusiasm incite the sprouting of the seed. But the triumph is short-lived as the seedling is exposed to the imperfect conditions of life. As the excitement fades, so does the seedling.

Have you ever experienced that fading away, dear reader? That joyless moment when you realize the excitement has completely disappeared. I have good news for you! You CAN overcome that feeling of despair, and regain and sustain the fervor you had for the initial planting of the word.

Connect with the father in your garden. In the quiet solitude, allow the words of his holy text to work their way into your heart. Read and meditate on the messages he leads you to. The silence will teach you more in one day than a lifetime of worldly voices. As those precious impartations work through the rocky soil, his seeds will again begin to germinate, only this time, the roots will grow strong and imperishable. Time spent in the garden, with Our Father, builds the soil of our hearts and frameworks the seedlings of promise.

The Lord said, as the farmer sowed, some seed fell among thorns which choked the young seedlings.

We all have thorns in our life, dear reader.

Thorns of worry and anxiety. Thorns of fret and fear. Thorns that torment us with thoughts of trouble and unease, distraction and disillusion.

Thorns prevent the germinated seed of God's holy word to grow and manifest into their full, fruitful potential.

We hear the word, we grow up with the word, we know the word, but the WORLD holds our hearts and hinders us from spending time in the garden.

Deep down in the intimate recesses of our souls, we understand the benevolence and beauty of the heavenly seed, but we allow the thorns of the world to rob us of this greatest treasure: time spent with our eternal father.

The Lord says in Daniel 12:4, "...many shall run to and fro, and knowledge shall increase."

The thorns of this world drown us in distraction through technology and media, business, employment, education, entertainment...some deemed avenues for knowledge and growth. Yet, as we race to and fro between these different paths, a common theme emerges: they are robbing us of time spent in the garden.

We must remove the thorns to allow space for the seed of God's word to grow. Decide who you're going to pursue, how and when you're going to schedule this meeting, and implement your plan. Simplicity is key. Start where you are at. I promise, dear reader, God will meet you there.

A friend of mine goes to the local convenience store every week, where she buys her favorite coffee. She then sits alone in her car and while enjoying her drink, she opens her bible to read and meditate on God's word. That is the garden she created. She lives in an urban area, works long, exhausting hours, and has little privacy in her home. When she decided to trade in some "thorns" and spend weekly time with God, her peace returned. Without her "garden time," life would devour her spiritually, mentally, physically and emotionally.

The Lord says in Proverbs 25:2, "It is the glory of God to conceal a matter, but the glory of kings is to search out a matter."

As we dig deeper in the garden, the meaning of God's word, and our revelation and understanding of his glorious plan for our life, will be exposed.

The Lord said, as the farmer sowed, other seed fell on good ground and yielded a crop: some a hundredfold, some sixty, some thirty. He who has ears to hear, let him hear!

This is the good news the Lord wants me to share, dear reader! Those whose hearts are prepared and ready to receive the holy seed of his word, will produce an abundant harvest!

The smallest of seed contains the greatest potential. Depending on the variety, one tiny tomato seed planted in good soil, can develop into a 5' plant which has the ability to produce up to 25 pounds of fruit!

Based on the meaning, one word from God, rooted and established in the soil of our hearts, has the potential to grow and produce an overwhelming crop of peace, or harvest of joy, or bushel basket of rest and relief.

Dear reader, I cannot emphasize enough the improved quality of your life resulting from time spent in the garden, tilling the soil, planting the seed, cultivating the most important relationship you will ever have: your bond with your heavenly father.

It's time to work on the soil of your heart.

Jennifer Garces

OBEDIENCE in the garden

1Samuel 15:22-23 ²² So Samuel said: "Has the Lord as great delight in burnt offerings and sacrifices, as in obeying the voice of the Lord? Behold, to obey is better than sacrifice, and to heed than the fat of rams. ²³ For rebellion is as the sin of witchcraft, and stubbornness is as iniquity and idolatry. Because you have rejected the word of the Lord, he also has rejected you from being king."

Do not despise correction.

Because of Saul's disobedience, he lost his crown.

He argued, though, that he did exactly what God had asked of him, EXCEPT for saving some choice animals to sacrifice to his Lord. Surely, that couldn't be a bad decision, or could it?

Who could forget what happened in the Garden of Eden. We live TODAY with the consequences of that calamitous mistake.

We call ourselves the most intelligent creatures on the planet. We label our race knowledgeable, learned, sophisticated, and highly evolved. Yet, we fall short of extending help, preserving justice, and promoting peace amongst one another. Our pride impels us to twist the truth and rewrite the sacred, to walk down forbidden paths out of rebellion. Disobedience leads to pain and destruction. God grieves, dear reader, when we ignore his guidance and direction. When we make the fatal decision to do things our way and not God's way. To amend and tweak his instruction to make things "right." After all, the world has changed. Surely, that couldn't be a bad thing, could it?

Throughout his Holy Word, God gives us clear and

direct instruction for living a life that is honorable and redemptive in his eyes. For our transgressions and iniquities, our generous Savior provides his grace; as we recognize and repent of our wrongdoings, he enables and equips us to overcome. Cliché as it sounds, I believe he simply wants us to do "our best" to follow his calling and counsel under all circumstances. However, because of our fallen, sinful nature, and the worldly pressures that suffocate us with conformity, being a "good Christian" can be a daunting task.

My challenge to you, dear reader, is to embrace a protocol of excellence in your thoughts, words, and deeds. My head bows as I write this. Immediately, a mirror of shame materializes and convicts me. This is difficult for me, dear reader! I am a sinner, not worthy of his love, undeserving of his ultimate sacrifice. I suddenly become so aware of the many instances of less-than-stellar behavior that color my existence. Excellence. An impossible challenge or call to something greater *(see Ephesians 2: 8-10)*?

I choose something greater. I encourage you to

choose something greater. It's within us. It's waiting for us to discover it. Something greater. God's supernatural strength and enablement. It's called Grace.

As you seek him, dear reader, as you visit the garden and walk with him in the cool of the day, I promise you that you WILL find what you are looking for and the world will never be the same.

Walk in his precepts and embrace his counsel. Allow his Spirit to invade the emptiness of your soul. Then, dear reader, you will experience the abundant life he has in store for you *(see John 10:10).*

Trust in the LORD with all your heart, and
lean not on your own understanding;
In all your ways acknowledge Him, and
He shall direct your paths.
Proverbs 3:5-6

Jennifer Garces

SEED in the garden

Luke 8:15 [15] But the ones that fell on the good ground are those who, having heard the word with a noble and good heart, keep it and bear fruit with patience.

Matthew 13:23 [23] But he who received seed on the good ground is he who hears the word and understands it, who indeed bears fruit and produces: some a hundredfold, some sixty, some thirty."

Which seed is planted in your heart? God's seed? Or the seed of this world?

Fruit is important to God because he is glorified when the seed of HIS holy word is planted inside of our hearts, is nurtured, flourishes, and produces an abundant harvest. When we share heaven's bounty, God's word is evangelized and planted in those we connect with.

God's seed is not easy to find in the world; it must be searched out. It is unique and rare.

The fruit produced from the seed of heaven is nourishing, self-sustaining, civilized and healthy for consumption. It reproduces reliably and true to form when planted in accordance with God's direction.

God's seed can remain dormant for decades; yet, when planted correctly, germinate and grow viable and strong.

Heaven's abundance and fruitfulness is satisfying for a lifetime, even passing on to future generations.

The seed of this world is less predictable and easier to access and attain. It roots speedily and grows quickly in the soul of the worldly granger. Although some worldly fruit may appear wholesome and carry some alimentary traits, it is not true to seed. In other words, it has been hybridized to conform to the wants and needs of the earthly sower. The fruit of this world, no matter how abundant, is fleeting and unpredictable. It may satisfy for a season, but not for a lifetime.

We are faced with significant choices every day, dear reader. Decisions that can and may affect the rest of our lives. We are continuously bombarded with seed of the world. Television, social media, news stories, publications, public schools, secular groups and institutions, our own government; all examples of people, places, and things that produce and spread worldly seed.

Be honest, dear reader. Are you allowing this type of seed to root into your heart and soul? Are you giving the messages of the world permission to sow into your destiny? Because once these plants of deception become established and you allow them to grow and produce fruit, the resulting harvest will smother and overtake God's seed.

Weeds, my dear reader, are difficult to control, especially if you allow them to root in, flourish, and produce more seed. Diligence is key. Remove the weeds as soon as possible. Turn off the distractions that do not line up with God's will. Even if the package looks appealing, remember, dear reader, the seeds of this world will only plant fear and disappointment, guilt and condemnation.

That's why you need the garden. That's why I need the garden. It is my secret, sacred place, created through God's hands, where I can decompress. Where I can safely release the seeds of this world without contaminating my heart. Here is where I recharge and recalibrate and restart the whole process of sowing heaven's seed into my heart.

Remember the hope he has for you *(see Jeremiah 29:11)*? The expectation he planted in your heart? The knowing that his thoughts for you are peaceful and focused on your future.

This is the reason, dear reader, for seeking the garden and using God's seed to plant a destiny designed around God's divine will for your life.

Jennifer Garces

HOPE in the garden

Jeremiah 29:11-13 "11 For I know the thoughts that I think toward you," says the Lord, "thoughts of peace and not of evil, to give you a future and a hope. 12 Then you will call upon Me and go and pray to Me, and I will listen to you. 13 And you will seek Me and find Me, when you search for Me with all your heart."

Do you repeatedly find yourself drowning in an endless torrent of distractions and to-do lists?

Life has become so scheduled. Work, school, appointments, playdates, sports practice, grocery shopping, homework…the list goes on and on. Very often, I find myself deep in distraction and I realize, dear reader, that what is most important to me has been overlooked, shelved, because of the "task bully." He is that little voice that keeps adding to your to-do list, that subtle internal murmur that guilts you into signing up your child for yet another after school activity, cons you into volunteering for another mindless cause, tricks you into missing another precious family dinner!

Guilt is a powerful weapon that the enemy wields with precision. He knows our weaknesses and like a 5-star general, he strikes repeatedly at our most vulnerable spots. Dear reader, **distraction becomes a tool of destruction in the hands of our enemy**. When we try to simplify and say "no" to the overwhelm, the enemy inflicts guilt and we inevitably cave in to the "opportunity."

What's one more class, right? Wrong.

All the commitments do is swallow up what IS important and purposeful in our lives; the callings on our heart from our loving Savior.

Without notice and like a thief in the night, eternal plans and designs are postponed, disabled, inactivated. We placate our self-disappointment and loathing by assuring ourselves that once we have more time and our schedules open up, we will return to God's calling on our hearts. But you and I know the truth, dear reader, that until WE take massive ACTION to control our schedule, the distractions will overwhelm and overtake us every time.

How do we escape these endless assaults on our time and scheduling?

Sometimes we need to go back to the beginning to reach our future.

Now is that time, dear reader.

But you cannot hear his voice until you turn off the volume of the world.

In the garden, you will find that quiet place. Your personal garden, or the park, sandy beach, mountains, botanical garden; any one of these places can serve as your Garden of Eden.

Turn off the cell phone and embrace the solitude.

God has a plan for you. A future filled with hope and thoughts of peace *(see Jeremiah 29:11)*. Receive Heaven's holy expectation, not just a "wish," but an understanding that God will come through for you in a design that is consistent with His word.

When you seek him with all your heart, you will find him *(see Jeremiah 29:13)* . His voice is small and still *(see 1Kings 19:12)* so by eliminating the "noise," disconnecting from the distractions, unplugging from the attacks on your senses, you are acting to regain control of your circumstances.

At first, it may take some concerted effort to evaluate and prioritize our schedules and to-do lists to plan these special appointment times in the garden.

Saying "no" is a learning process for many of us!

As you call upon the Lord, and you pray and seek him with all your heart, he will listen and answer *(see Psalm 50:15)*. The mountains of distraction will dissipate and the Lord will restore the peace that you lost in the deluge of despair.

HOPE will return, dear reader, as you disengage from the world and reconnect with him in your garden.

Jennifer Garces

ROOTS in the garden

Jeremiah 17:7-8 [7]Blessed is the man who trusts in the LORD, And whose hope is the LORD. [8]For he shall be like a tree planted by the waters, Which spreads out its roots by the river, And will not fear when heat comes; But its leaf will be green, And will not be anxious in the year of drought, Nor will cease from yielding fruit.

Roots are the most important part of the plant. They feed, nourish, anchor, and sustain the entire tree. Root vitality dictates the health, stability, and fruitfulness of the tree.

What is interesting and unique about the roots of a plant is the fact they are hidden; enveloped in soil. Because they are not visible, their importance is often overlooked, and the impact on the overall health and vigor of the tree is neglected.

When attention is focused only on what is visible, unexpected problems can occur. Dear reader, how many times have you looked at someone and thought how physically attractive, stable, and happy they appeared. Yet later on, were informed they suffered with terrible anxiety, stress, and dysfunction. Eventually, what is manifesting on the inside, internally, will work its way to the outside, or the exterior.

Another unnoticed fact is that roots need a nourishing soil to supply and bolster their needs. Good, healthy soil promotes strong root growth and establishment.

A profound synergy exists between soil and roots.

The Garden of Your Heart

The deeper your roots grow, the stronger your faith, the greater your trust, the more enduring your hope.

The Lord said in Job 14: 7-9, "7 For there is hope for a tree, if it is cut down, that it will sprout again, and that its tender shoots will not cease. 8 Though its root may grow old in the earth, and its stump may die in the ground, 9 Yet at the scent of water it will bud and bring forth branches like a plant."

You see, dear reader, that even if our physical appearance deteriorates and begins to fade, the roots of our faith, hope, and enduring trust will sustain us, until the regrowth of our Glory through Jesus our Savior.

A tree may die over the course of a severe winter season. However, if the roots are strong, new growth will emerge as the soil receives the spring rains and sunshine. A brand new tree – bigger, healthier and more vibrant – will begin to grow. As a part of us dies back from the storms of life, our roots in Christ will stimulate new and advanced growth; often, we flourish and produce our greatest harvest after the tribulation.

Grow your roots strong, dear reader, as you spend time in the garden with Father God. Invite his presence to saturate the seed he has planted in your heart. Give your garden the time needed to grow deep and sustaining roots in his holy scripture.

The Lord wants you to flourish, dear reader.

May your heart be firmly rooted in faith,
trust and hope as you begin the journey of growing
your own Garden of Life.

Jennifer Garces

FAITH in the garden

I know you're able and I know You can, save through the fire with your mighty hand, But even if you don't, My hope is you alone. MercyMe

Oh My soul, You are not alone, There's a place where fear has to face the God you know. Casting Crowns

Ephesians 2:8...by grace you have been saved through faith, and that not of yourselves; it is the gift of God.

Faith is an action. A choice. Faith comes by hearing the word of God *(see Romans 10:17)*, the life-giving seed he instills in our hearts and souls. When everything is crumbling around you, faith keeps you.

As life delivers its blows and sends you reeling, the words of God are there for you to hold onto. To meditate and lay hold of. Your allegiance to his promises will instill peace in your soul and strength in your body.

But what happens, dear readers, when he doesn't deliver as expected? Disappointment. Despair. A feeling of betrayal from our greatest love. That's when faith must supersede every emotion including heartache.

As the tears are flowing, dear reader, lift your hands to heaven and release those tears to him. Give him your pain and sadness; cry out to him! He is listening, dear reader. God LOVES you! He is the man of sorrows and his greatest desire is to comfort you and give you rest. His burden is light and his yoke is easy. He doesn't want us to carry the crushing weight of this world.

When deliverance doesn't come. When the healing doesn't take place. God enables us, through his endless gift of heavenly grace, to hold on and overcome. Our faith activates the ability to move mountains *(see Matthew 17:20 below)*. And we can pray, dear readers, when our faith is wavering and our hearts are wrenched inside of us, for God to step in and make a way where it appears there is none. We can plead for God to take the tattered pieces of faith that sprinkle our souls and knit them together to form an impenetrable barrier of grace and strength.

A mustard seed is a tiny object. That's all the faith we need for God to do a work within us and through us. *In Matthew 17:20, the Lord said, "Because you have so little faith. Truly I tell you, if you have faith as small as a mustard seed, you can say to this mountain, 'Move from here to there,' and it will move. Nothing will be impossible for you."* God said that through FAITH, **nothing will be impossible for you.** Choose faith, dear reader. Live in faith. Speak in faith. Believe in faith. It is your gift, from the God above, to equip and enable you to overcome this world.

Jennifer Garces

SEASONS in the garden

Ecclesiastes 3:1-2 [1] To everything there is a season, A time for every purpose under heaven: [2] A time to be born, and a time to die; A time to plant, and a time to pluck what is planted.

Winter. A dormant season. Barrenness. Quiet desolation. Sleep envelops the garden. The vibrant green of summer and autumn has long been replaced by colorless, lifeless forms of grey and brown and dry straw. A haze of white frost covers the vegetative corpses in a frosty blanket. Death is everywhere. This lifeless atmosphere brings me into a depressive state of hopelessness. If I wasn't sure that Spring would eventually arrive, I might succumb to madness!

The winter seasons of stark discontent can be a curse, or a blessing. Our response and reaction determines our choice. Yes, dear reader, we can choose how to receive the season we are experiencing.

Often, we are powerless to change our circumstances, however, we do possess the ability to change our interpretation and emotional reaction to any given condition.

Look at the garden in winter, dear reader. If you don't KNOW the garden, it appears dead. Gone. Forever. But if you know the CREATOR of the garden, his handiwork, his cycles, you would understand that the garden is merely hibernating. Sleeping. Readying itself for another season of growth, flourishment, and fruitfulness.

Faith gives you eyes to see what isn't yet visible *(see Hebrews 11:1).*

Trust gives you peace to know that winter is not a temporary setback, but a time of complete rest.

Hope gives you expectancy for the advancement God is preparing.

Spring. An awakening season. Joy. Resurrection. What appeared dead now bursts into life. The blank color of winter is now overtaken by greens and blues and pinks and whites. The quiet is replaced by jubilant bird songs, singing their happiness through worship. The sleepers awake and the sun bathes the fertility in bright, golden light.

It is a time of jubilee. Victory. The garden slowly begins to awaken. The seeds that were left behind by the last harvest germinate, and spread the good news of life.

Summer. A flourishing season. Abundant growth. Blooms. Beauty. Also, a time to watch and wait upon. As prolific growth emerges, so does the unwanted verdure. Separation of weeds and cultivated plants is necessary.

Pests. Heat. Rain – too much or too little. Maintenance is required. Watchfulness and action is mandatory to keep the garden healthy and bountiful.

Summer is a season of activity. So much to enjoy, but not without defense and preservation. Dear reader, remember, guard your hearts *(see Proverbs 4:23)* and minds through prayer and thanksgiving. Especially when you are in a season of expansion. We have an enemy who would thoroughly enjoy spoiling every plan and purpose God has for you.

Fall. A season of fruitfulness. Abundance. Harvest. My favorite time of year. Cool nights and warm days. Perfect blue skies painted with cottony white clouds.

As the garden begins to wind down, the wild animals collect and store their winter meals. Many winged creatures head south to escape. They know the season that follows Autumn, and an inner drive prompts them to prepare.

The Fall is a season of preparation. An

appointed period designated for us to get our houses in order. It is a time of grace and giving. Our God supplies all our needs according to his riches *(see Philippians 4:19)*. If we respond to the season accordingly, we will not welcome lack when it comes knocking at our door. Harvest time represents God's provision.

Fall is the season where we reap what we sow *(see Galatians 6:7)*. It represents the manifestation of the seed that we have sown into our hearts. I pray, dear reader, that you reap fruit from God's seed and not from the world's. Fall is a season of actuality and conviction. Fruit does not lie. It is the undeniable expression of the seed that bore it.

The Fall season brings truth and clarity. Embrace the reality of this season, dear reader. And please know this: the garden is FORGIVING. Every Spring, we all have the absolute fortune to plant new seed. Life seed. God's seed.

Live and learn through the seasons that God places us in, dear reader. They are all blessings in their appointed times.

.

TRIALS in the garden

2Timothy 4:5-8 "5But you be watchful in all things, endure afflictions, do the work of an evangelist, fulfill your ministry. 6 For I am already being poured out as a drink offering, and the time of my departure is at hand. 7 I have fought the good fight, I have finished the race, I have kept the faith. 8 Finally, there is laid up for me the crown of righteousness, which the Lord, the righteous Judge, will give to me on that Day, and not to me only but also to all who have loved His appearing."

Whoever said he promised us a rose garden

without thorns?

Trials, my dear reader, are part of life. We know and understand this. As followers of the Most High God, we understand that exemptions from suffering are not included in our earthly salvation.

Suffering and trials do not originate from God's hand, but he does use and allow unsavory circumstances to develop and increase our faith. Trials provide opportunities for spiritual growth. Often, all we can do to endure a situation is to completely trust God. In our weakest state, helpless and fully dependent on God's intervention, his power is perfected and his GRACE is sufficient (*see 2Corinthians 12:9*).

God will carry us through every situation when we trust and surrender our heaviest burdens to him.

Through trials, our relationship with God deepens and grows. Our dependence on the Almighty matures into a collaboration of trust and certainty. Although the winter sky is cold and void of any color, we trust the spring rains and warmth will entice the tree blossoms to grow and burst at the right time. Trials teach us to wait. Patiently. God's timing is always perfect. Suffering builds our character and develops our gratitude skills. Thankfulness for all that is right in our world. Thanksgiving brings an atmosphere of hope to a situation, an accelerator to propel the future into our present state.

More often than not, the reasons for our tribulations elude us. But the response, dear readers, to the trials that come our way determines the outcome.

In my own life, dear reader, God used unpleasant situations to expose my own unloving attitudes and beliefs. The fire purged and purified and brought me closer to the cross. Because I was so desperate for God, and he loved me so much, he allowed painful circumstances to surface in order to prepare me to sit at his right hand.

But he never gave me a cross that was too heavy to bear. And he placed angels in my midst to minister, protect and strengthen me.

We have a choice. To allow our disappointment and anger to separate us from our Savior. Or, to embrace God's sovereign presence in the midst of our storm; to fully surrender our heartache and hopelessness in exchange for his guidance, strength, and heavenly peace.

The choice is ours.

We do have this absolute promise, dear readers: our Lord and Savior will NEVER leave us nor forsake us *(see Hebrews 13:5).*

We can trust and rest in that word today and always.

Heaven's War Room is the Garden.

Kim Clement

Jennifer Garces

HARVEST in the garden

Galatians 6:7-9 [7] Do not be deceived, God is not mocked; for whatever a man sows, that he will also reap. [8] For he who sows to his flesh will of the flesh reap corruption, but he who sows to the Spirit will of the Spirit reap everlasting life. [9] And let us not grow weary while doing good, for in due season we shall reap if we do not lose heart.

Isaiah 61:3 [3] To console those who mourn in Zion, to give them beauty for ashes, the oil of joy for mourning, the garment of praise for the spirit of heaviness; that they may be called trees of righteousness, the planting of the Lord, that He may be glorified.

You shall reap what you sow.

How many times have you heard, or said that, dear reader? A profound but simple truth that many cultures and religions have adopted over millennium.

Harvest is the result of a lifetime of preparing, cultivating, planting, and growing that which God has entrusted to us... in us... and through us. Do not be mistaken, dear reader, God has been planting seeds within us throughout our entire life.

Some seeds have taken decades to germinate, sprouting so slowly that we weren't even aware they were there. But God's word never returns void *(see Isaiah 55:11)*, dear reader.

When the soil is ready and the conditions are in alignment, growth begins.

However, that seed of potential that exists within you cannot grow until God has plowed and tilled and prepared the soil of your heart.

Please give God the opportunity, dear reader, to

work on your heart. The Savior LONGS to create a stunning and abundant garden of life within you. He is the creator of your whole being, the master artist who paints your world in amazing colors of joy and peace, love and victory. When you give the Lord your time in the garden, he shows up and walks with you in the cool of the day *(see Genesis 3:8)*. Refreshment and restoration is yours when you invite the Savior to enter into your garden.

My heart breaks for you, dear reader, because I know some of you are too broken, too hurt, too injured to open your garden gate. You hold onto your hardened hearts to shield and protect yourselves from further violation.

The Lord understands, dear reader.

God sees your tears and he holds every single one in the palms of his loving, nurturing hands.

God brought you here, to these words, to let you know that you are not alone.

GOD KNOWS YOU.

AND GOD LOVES YOU.

His greatest desire is to enter into your heart and oh so gently, begin the process of creating a beautiful and fruitful garden.

Won't you invite the master gardener into your heart, dear reader?

And let us not grow weary while doing good, for in due season we shall reap if we do not lose heart.

Galatians 6:9

Jennifer Garces

RETRIBUTION in the garden

2Corinthians 9:6 "⁶But this I say: He who sows sparingly will also reap sparingly, and he who sows bountifully will also reap bountifully."

Proverbs 1:31 Therefore they shall eat the fruit of their own way, and be filled to the full with their own fancies.

When I saw the word retribution, dear reader, I immediately envisioned another word: "payback."

A scary thought for a sinner like me!

Far from perfect, full of remorse and shame, I

didn't believe God wanted anything to do with me, let alone use me to minister and encourage others! My prayers consisted of tearful pleadings for mercy and forgiveness. I felt so unholy and stained.

But my hunger was ravenous. I wanted him. I wanted to know GOD.

I NEEDED TO KNOW IF HE REALLY LOVED ME THE WAY THAT I WAS.

I read my prayer books from memory.

I cried out for help!

Waiting in the pews more mornings than I can remember and praying out loud with no voice. Crying inside for someone, anyone, to hear me or see me. I felt invisible.

NOTHING.

Where are you, God? Why aren't you here?

I was like a lost sheep, alone in the wilderness, trying to find her shepherd.

The more I searched, the deeper the silence. The truth was, I didn't feel loved or understood or even acceptable. Even worse, I began to think perhaps I was looking for something that didn't exist.

And then the unexpected happened; a massive storm suddenly descended upon our family.

My health failed shortly after the birth of our third child. Surgery was impending. At the same time, unwarranted legal problems plagued our business. The ruthless attacks on our company and my health wreaked havoc on my fragile heart and completely disrupted my entire family.

My God, why have you forsaken me?

I was so lost and broken, dear reader. My desire to find God was shattered into a million disappointed pieces. Life was too hard and I didn't want to do it alone anymore. Not without him.

But God heard my cry.....

Having lost almost all hope and faith, God sent me

a messenger; my modern day "Mary." A loving, brazen, Spirit-filled soul who boldly prayed life back into my dry, dead bones. As she declared victory and commanded the enemy to "get off her friend," something shifted in my spirit.

In the deepest, darkest place, suddenly there was a small but very bright light.

In God's perfect and anointed timing *(see Ecclesiastes 3:1)*, he showed up. As I searched him with all my heart *(see Jeremiah 29:13)*, I began to hear the still, small voice *(1Kings 19:12)*. The subtle messages that fit together like puzzle pieces to create a beautiful and inspiring portrait.

During that incredible growing season, the message that God instilled in my heart was:

"My grace is sufficient for you, for My strength is made perfect in weakness." (2Corinthians 12:9)

My heart had been so hard, dear reader, so compacted and trodden by religion, rejection, pain, and disappointment.

But God met me exactly where I was at.

When all I heard was deafening silence, Jesus my Savior was quietly weeding and plowing and cultivating the wretched soil of my heart. My hunger and pursuit of him activated his loving, steadfast presence in my life.

But the process didn't happen overnight, dear reader. It takes time to prepare the garden of your heart.

God had to first teach me about TRUST.

When I was at my weakest, when I was face down, crying out in despair and confusion, his GRACE was sufficient. When I lost my will, the POWER of his love came in and rescued me!

He saved me from the world, and myself, dear reader!

God wants you to know that he is NOT a God who seeks retribution! Please, dear reader, understand that he IS a God of love and mercy, grace and kindness, forgiveness and redemption. Only our Savior redeems us from our sins and offers us life eternal.

Jesus already paid the price for our sin on the cross at Calvary. We have been made clean by his atonement over two thousand years ago.

When I cried out to my heavenly daddy, when I called on him from my garden of despair, he HEARD me and he answered me. He didn't look at the weeds, and the thorns, the tangle of fruitless messiness; he responded to my heart cry. My God saw something beautiful beneath the overgrowth of worldliness!

Because of his love, I no longer feel abandoned and ashamed. God has restored my heart and planted seeds of hope and strength, triumph and joy, peace and prosperity. The garden of my heart has grown so abundantly that I am now able to share my harvest, with you, dear reader! And that is the GREATEST gift that I can give back to my heavenly father.

You see, dear reader, my harvest was not grown just for me. The harvest from the garden of my heart was grown for YOU.

The Garden of Your Heart

That you might know his great LOVE for you.

Jennifer Garces

REVELATION in the garden

Matthew 7: 13-14 "[13]Enter by the narrow gate; for wide is the gate and broad is the way that leads to destruction, and there are many who go in by it. [14] Because narrow is the gate and difficult is the way which leads to life, and there are few who find it."

Where is your path leading you? To God? Or away from God?

I share and express the feelings, thoughts, and emotions that are stirring within me so that, dear reader, you might be infected with a desire to cultivate your own Garden of Eden, your personal Genesis experience.

We all possess a longing in our souls, an emptiness that aches for something real and lasting. When I work in my garden, when I place those tiny, fragile seeds into the soil and I gently cover them, a feeling of hope and renewal washes over me. My faith activates within my soul and I see the future; precious, little seedlings poking through the soil, reaching towards the sunlight. The beauty and miracle of life. The fulfillment of progress. The blessing of simple, yet profound abundance.

Be a blessing to yourself, dear reader. Decide today how you're going to pursue and cultivate your own Garden of Eden. You owe it to your spiritual health and physical wellbeing. By investing in your destiny, you are preparing the soil of your heart to receive and germinate your own seeds from heaven.

As you progress and the fruits of your labor produce, you will have the ability to share your own seed to build the Kingdom here on earth!

The Garden of Your Heart

Feel the hunger within you? You are not alone. So many parched, dry souls walking the earth, deafened by the noise and distractions of the world. Beaten down by the storms of life. Starved for simplicity and solitude.

My Garden of Eden became my place of rest and healing. I was wounded. Deeply. And I needed to touch heaven and feel God's loving and restorative grace. He met me in the garden. We walked in the cool of the day. My Savior sat with me as I planted the seeds and my shattered heart began to mend. My joy returned. My soul was no longer parched and empty of life. I began to grow and flourish and produce my own seeds of life and abundance.

This little book represents a portion of the harvest that manifested from the tears that watered the seed God planted in my heart. MY tears. The tears that my Savior, Jesus, still holds in the palms of his holy hands.

Psalm 126:5 says, those who sow in tears, shall reap in joy.

I do not possess a barn big enough, dear reader, to

store the abounding harvest of joy that is my portion *(see Psalm 28:7)*! GOD is so very, very GOOD.

Dear reader, know without a doubt that you are loved, and allow that divine insight to put you on the path that leads to God and the abundant life he has purposed for you.

Narrow is the gate and difficult is the way which
leads to life, and there are few who find it.
Matthew 7:14

Jennifer Garces

INVITATION *to the garden*

*Matthew 11:28-30 "²⁸Come to Me, all you who labor and are heavy laden, and I will give you **rest**. ²⁹Take My yoke upon you and learn from Me, for I am **gentle** and lowly in heart, and you will find rest for your souls. ³⁰For My yoke is easy and My burden is light."*

Isaiah 58:11 And the LORD will continually guide you, and satisfy your desire in scorched places, and give strength to your bones; and you will be like a watered garden, and like a spring of water whose waters do not fail.

Would you like to invite God into the garden of

your heart, dear reader?

Be not afraid, for my God, YOUR God, OUR GOD is waiting with open arms to accept your invitation.

He says, "Come as you are, dear child. When I look at you, all I see is beauty and I long to sow love and restoration, healing and grace, peace and joy into your heart. Please give me the opportunity to be your forever father."

Dear Lord Jesus, I believe you truly are the Son of God, that you died on the cross to deliver me from my sin and offer me eternal salvation with you in glorious heaven. Because you have forgiven me, I choose to forgive myself, and follow you as my eternal Father and Savior. Rule and reign in my heart and fill it with your love and life. Restore me, Lord God, and plant something beautiful in me.

In Jesus' name I pray, Amen.

Jennifer Garces

ABOUT THE AUTHOR

Jennifer Garces is an avid garden strategist whose passion revolves around creating and cultivating extraordinary landscapes. During difficult seasons in her life, she's found restoration and healing through intimate prayer in her private garden. Jennifer's desire is to show people how to grow a deeper relationship with God through the garden, while flourishing in abundant joy and a faith-filled harvest.

She is happily married 20 years and has three homeschooled teenagers, two dogs, several cats, and a henhouse full of chickens.

Jennifer grows and harvests from her organic vegetable garden, has a small orchard of 25 apple trees, and pre-serves her own salsa, ratatouille, and tomato sauce for her family and friends to enjoy.

Jennifer Garces

90195227R10051

Made in the USA
Lexington, KY
08 June 2018